PIANO FUN ROMANTIC HITS FOR ADULT BEGINNERS

Arranged by Brenda Dillon

CONTENTS

	PAGE
Performance Notes	2
Can't Help Falling in Love	
Lead Sheet	6
Arrangement	26
Days of Wine and Roses	
Lead Sheet	7
Arrangement	28
Dear Heart	
Lead Sheet	8
Arrangement	30
Here's That Rainy Day	
Lead Sheet	9
Arrangement	32
It Was Almost Like a Song	
Lead Sheet	10
Arrangement	34
Jean	
Lead Sheet	12
Arrangement	37
My Romance	
Lead Sheet	14
Arrangement	40

	PAGE
The Shadow of Your Smile	
Lead Sheet	15
Arrangement	42
Smile	
Lead Sheet	16
Arrangement	44
Some Day My Prince Will Come	
Lead Sheet	17
Arrangement	46
Sunshine on My Shoulders	
Lead Sheet	18
Arrangement	54
Unchained Melody	
Lead Sheet	20
Arrangement	48
The Way We Were	
Lead Sheet	22
Arrangement	50
Yesterday	
Lead Sheet	21
Arrangement	52

To access audio visit:
www.halleonard.com/mylibrary

Enter Code
6163-1608-3803-2044

ISBN 978-1-4803-9711-8

HAL•LEONARD®
CORPORATION

7777 W. BLUEMOUND RD. P.O. BOX 13819 MILWAUKEE, WI 53213

Visit Hal Leonard Online at
www.halleonard.com

PERFORMANCE NOTES

Introduction

Welcome to *Piano Fun: Romantic Hits for Adult Beginners,* a collection of lead sheets and arrangements for the beginning pianist who has learned how to read music and wants to play easy arrangements of familiar melodies.

About the Orchestrations

The orchestrations are recorded on two tracks – a slow track with the melody and a slightly faster track without the melody. The orchestrator is Will Baily, composer and Recreational Music Making (RMM) facilitator who has been composing and orchestrating specifically for RMM students of all ages for the past six years. He has presented at the MTNA conference and on MTNA's Pedagogy Saturday. A former college professor, Will operates a large RMM studio in Scottsbluff, NE, that serves approximately 300 students of all ages.

Triads/Chords

- Triads are three-note chords. The bottom note is the root, the next note above is the 3rd, and the top note is the 5th.

- Major triads can be altered to become minor, diminished, or augmented.

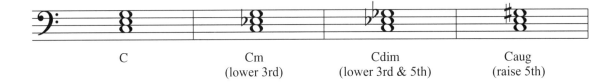

- Seventh chords are spelled with four notes. The bottom note is the root, the next note above is the 3rd, the note above the 3rd is the 5th, and the top note is the 7th.

- Major 7th chords can be altered to become dominant 7th, minor 7th, and diminished 7th.

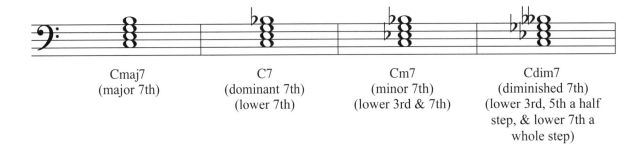

- Added 6th chords are four note chords that include the root, 3rd, 5th, and a 6th above the root.

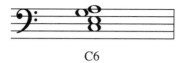

C6

- A chord can also have a suspension which usually resolves to one of the regular chord tones. A Csus4 suspension has a 4th above C (F) which resolves to E in the following chord.

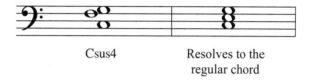

Csus4   Resolves to the
regular chord

- An example of a 7th chord with a suspension is A7sus4. The chord without the suspension is spelled A C♯ E G. With a sus4, the chord is spelled A D E G. The 4th (D) then resolves to the 3rd (C♯).

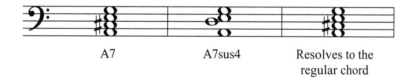

A7   A7sus4   Resolves to the
regular chord

LEAD SHEETS

Can't Help Falling in Love

from the Paramount Picture BLUE HAWAII

Words and Music by George David Weiss,
Hugo Peretti and Luigi Creatore
Arranged by Brenda Dillon

Days of Wine and Roses

from DAYS OF WINE AND ROSES

Lyrics by Johnny Mercer
Music by Henry Mancini
Arranged by Brenda Dillon

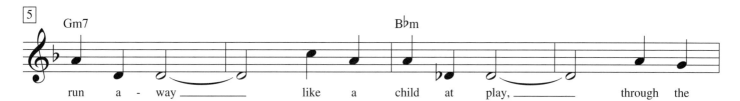

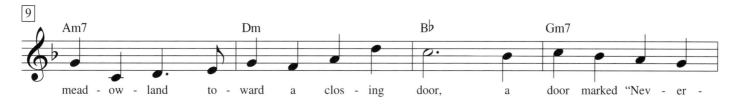

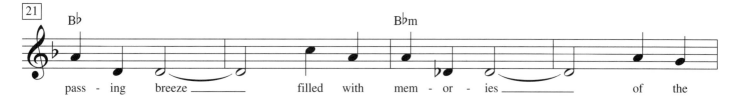

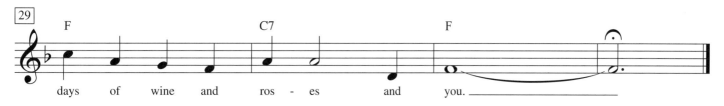

Dear Heart
from DEAR HEART

Music by Henry Mancini
Words by Jay Livingston and Ray Evans
Arranged by Brenda Dillon

Here's That Rainy Day
from CARNIVAL IN FLANDERS

Words by Johnny Burke
Music by Jimmy Van Heusen

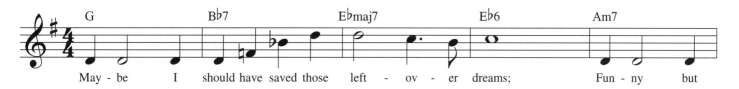

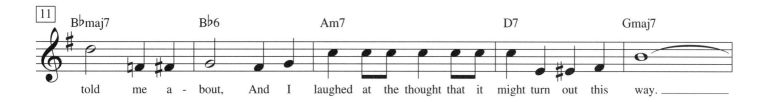

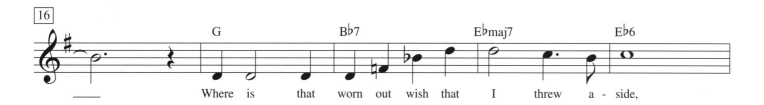

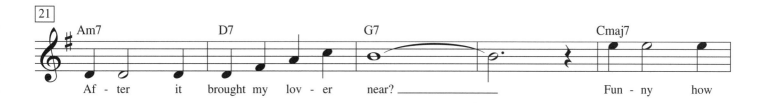

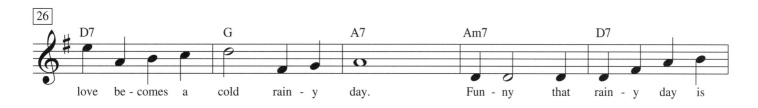

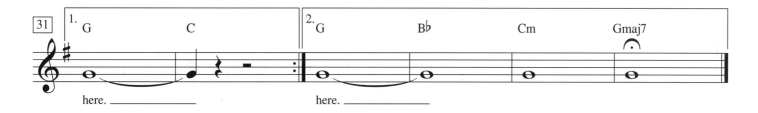

It Was Almost Like a Song

Lyric by Hal David
Music by Archie Jordan
Arranged by Brenda Dillon

Once in ev - 'ry life,   some - one comes a - long,

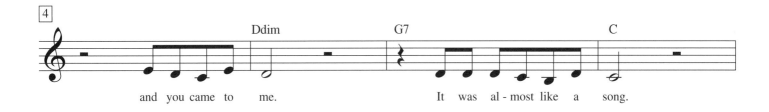

and you came to me.   It was al - most like a song.

You were in my arms,   just where you be - long,

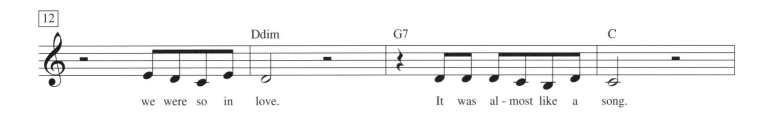

we were so in love.   It was al - most like a song.

Jan - u - ar - y through De - cem - ber,   we had such a per - fect

year; Then the flame be - came a dy - ing em - ber; all at once you weren't

there. Now my brok - en heart cries for you each

night. It's al - most like a song, — but it's too sad to

write. Now my brok - en heart cries for you each

night. It's al - most like a song. — But it's too sad to

write. It's too sad to write. _____

Jean

Words and Music by
Rod McKuen
Arranged by Brenda Dillon

Jean, Jean, ros - es are red, all the

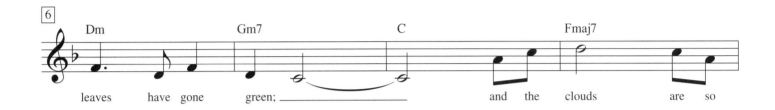

leaves have gone green; _____ and the clouds are so

low, you can touch them and so come out to the

mead - ow Jean. Jean, Jean, you're

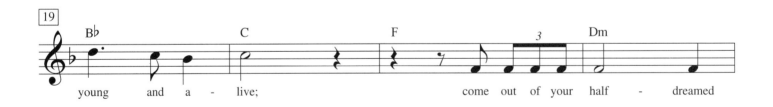

young and a - live; come out of your half - dreamed

dream _____ and run, if you will, to the top of the

hill; _____ o - pen your arms, bon - nie Jean. _____

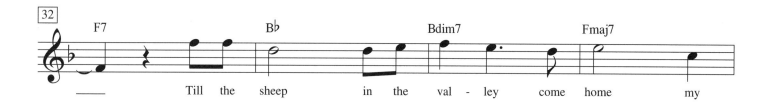

____ Till the sheep in the val - ley come home my

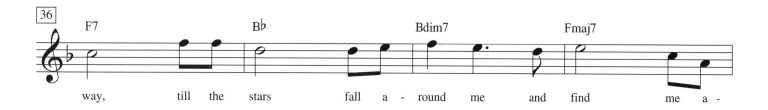

way, till the stars fall a - round me and find me a -

lone, when the sun comes a sing - in', I'll still be

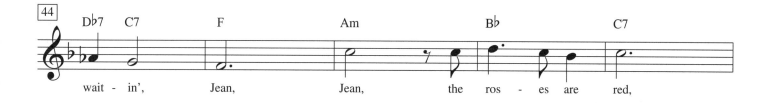

wait - in', Jean, Jean, the ros - es are red,

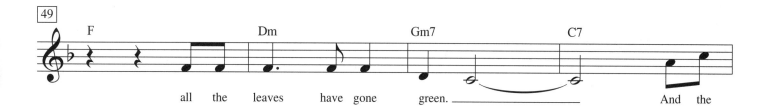

all the leaves have gone green. _____ And the

hills are a - blaze with the moon's yel - low haze;

come in - to my arms, bon - nie Jean.

13

My Romance
from JUMBO

Words by Lorenz Hart
Music by Richard Rodgers
Arranged by Brenda Dillon

My ro- mance does-n't have to have a moon in the sky. My ro-

mance does-n't need a blue la- goon stand- ing by; No

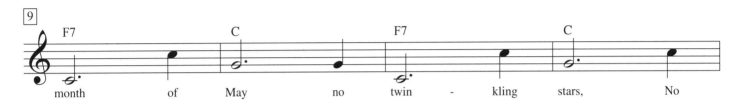

month of May no twin- kling stars, No

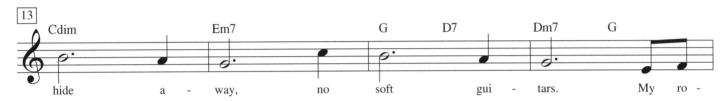

hide a- way, no soft gui- tars. My ro-

mance does-n't need a cas- tle ris- ing in Spain, Nor a

dance to a con- stant- ly sur- pris- ing re- frain. Wide a-

wake I can make my most fan- tas- tic dreams come true; My ro-

mance does-n't need a thing but you. _____

The Shadow of Your Smile
Love Theme from THE SANDPIPER

Music by Johnny Mandel
Words by Paul Francis Webster
Arranged by Brenda Dillon

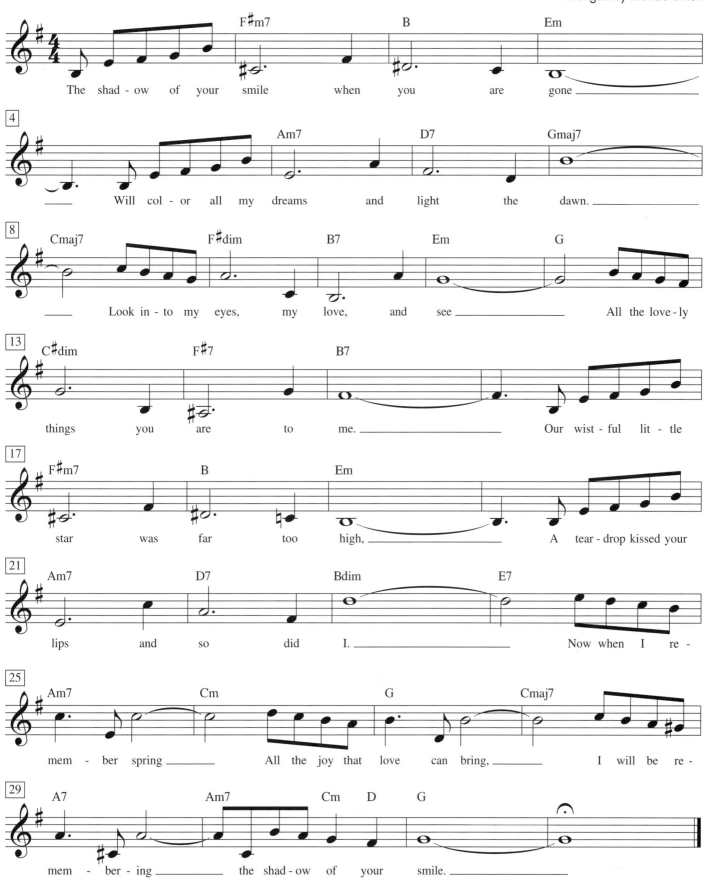

Smile
Theme from MODERN TIMES

Words by John Turner and Geoffrey Parsons
Music by Charles Chaplin

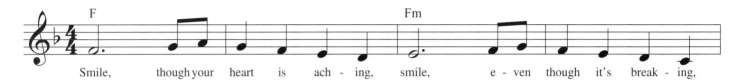

Smile, though your heart is ach - ing, smile, e - ven though it's break - ing,

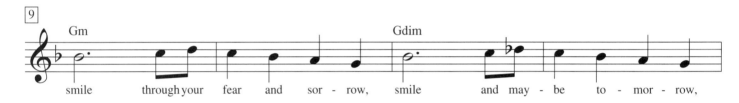

When there are clouds in the sky, you'll get by, if you

smile through your fear and sor - row, smile and may - be to - mor - row,

you'll see the sun comes shin - ing through for you. Light up your

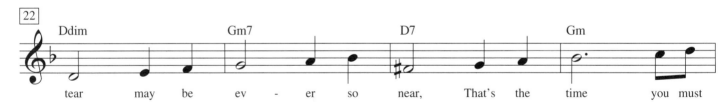

face with glad - ness, Hide ev - 'ry trace of sad - ness, Al - though a

tear may be ev - er so near, That's the time you must

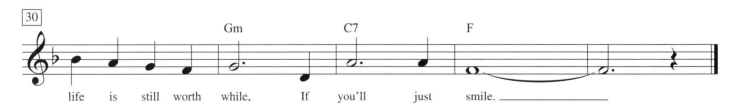

keep on try - ing, smile, what's the use of cry - ing, you'll find that

life is still worth while, If you'll just smile. _____

Some Day My Prince Will Come

Words by Larry Morey
Music by Frank Churchill

Some day my prince will come, some day I'll

find my love, and how thrill - ing that mo - ment will be. _____

_____ When the Prince of my dreams comes to me, _____

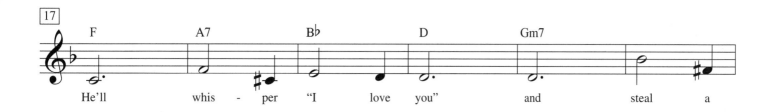

He'll whis - per "I love you" and steal a

kiss or two. Though he's far a - way, I'll find my love some

day. Some day when my dreams come true. _____

Sunshine on My Shoulders

Words by John Denver
Music by John Denver,
Mike Taylor and Dick Kniss
Arranged by Brenda Dillon

Sun - shine _____ on my shoul - ders _____ makes me hap - py, _____

sun - shine _____ in my eyes can make me cry. _____

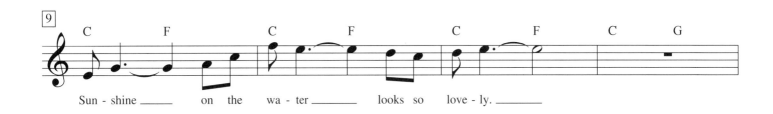

Sun - shine _____ on the wa - ter _____ looks so love - ly. _____

Sun - shine _____ al - most al - ways _____ makes me high. _____

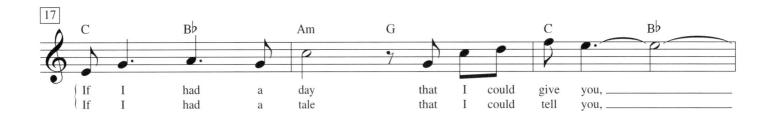

If I had a day that I could give you, _____
If I had a tale that I could tell you, _____

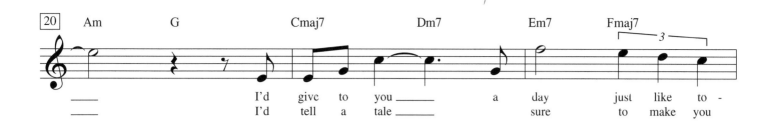

20 | Am | G | Cmaj7 | Dm7 | Em7 | Fmaj7

_____ I'd give to you _____ a day just like to -
_____ I'd tell a tale _____ sure to make you

23 | Dm7 | G7 | C | B♭ | Am | G

day. _____ If I had _____ a song that I could
smile. _____ If I had _____ a wish that I could

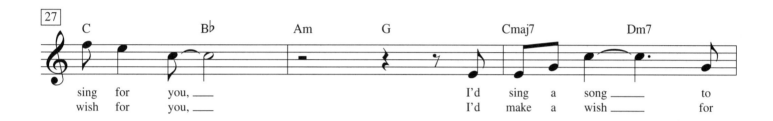

27 | C | B♭ | Am | G | Cmaj7 | Dm7

sing for you, _____ I'd sing a song _____ to
wish for you, _____ I'd make a wish _____ for

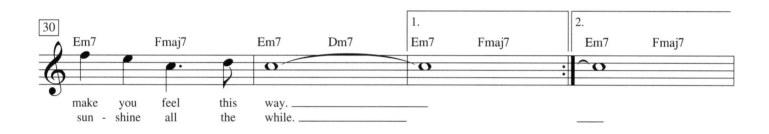

30 | Em7 | Fmaj7 | Em7 | Dm7 | 1. Em7 Fmaj7 | 2. Em7 Fmaj7

make you feel this way. _____
sun - shine all the while. _____ _____

34 | C | F | C | F | Cmaj7 Dm7 Em7 Dm7

Sun - shine _____ al - most all the time makes me high, _____

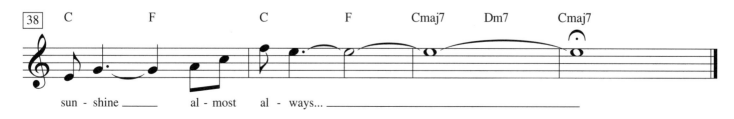

38 | C | F | C | F | Cmaj7 Dm7 Cmaj7

sun - shine _____ al - most al - ways... _____

Unchained Melody

Lyric by Hy Zaret
Music by Alex North
Arranged by Brenda Dillon

Oh, my love, my dar - ling, I've hun - gered for your

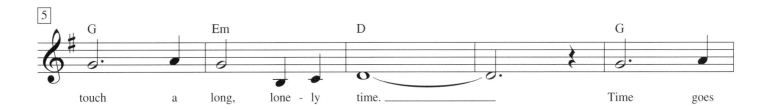

touch a long, lone - ly time. _____ Time goes

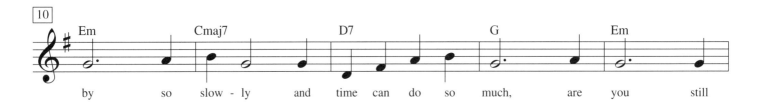

by so slow - ly and time can do so much, are you still

mine? _____ I need your love, _____ I need your love, _____

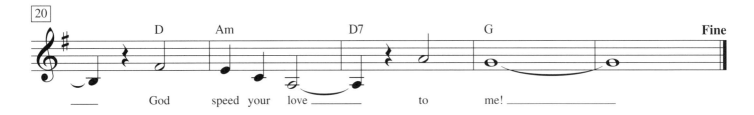

_____ God speed your love _____ to me!

Lone - ly riv - ers flow to the sea, to the sea. To the o - pen
Lone - ly riv - ers sigh, "Wait for me, wait for me!" I'll be com - ing

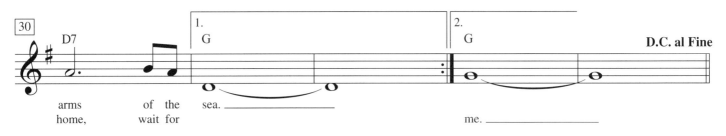

arms of the sea. _____
home, wait for   me. _____

Yesterday

Words and Music by John Lennon
and Paul McCartney
Arranged by Brenda Dillon

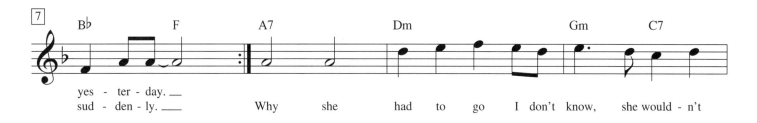

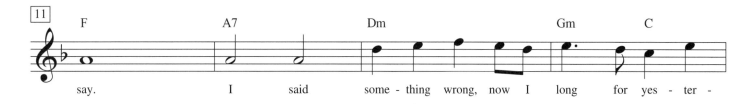

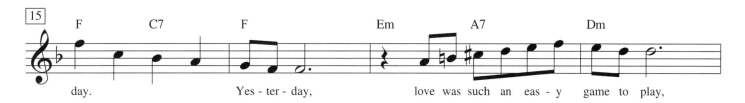

The Way We Were

from the Motion Picture THE WAY WE WERE

Words by Alan and Marilyn Bergman
Music by Marvin Hamlisch
Arranged by Brenda Dillon

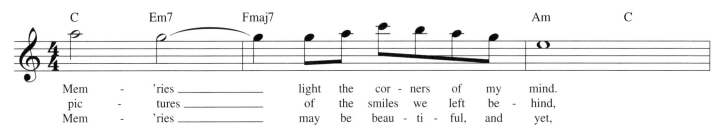

Mem - 'ries _____ light the cor - ners of my mind.
pic - tures _____ of the smiles we left be - hind,
Mem - 'ries _____ may be beau - ti - ful, and yet,

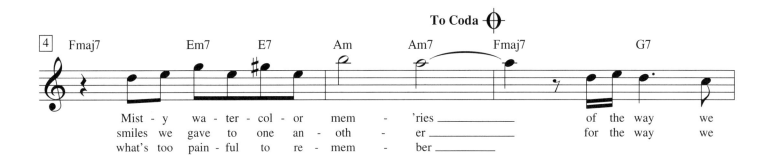

Mist - y wa - ter - col - or mem - 'ries _____ of the way we
smiles we gave to one an - oth - er _____ for the way we
what's too pain - ful to re - mem - ber _____

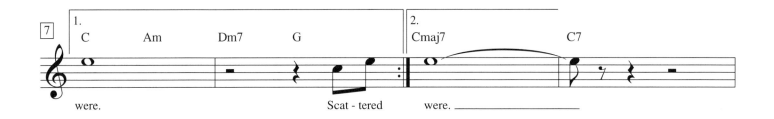

were. Scat - tered were. _____

Can it be that it was all so sim - ple then, or has time re - writ - ten ev - 'ry

14 | Asus A Dm7 Em7 Dm7 G7

linc? If wc had thc chancc to do it all a - gain, tell me

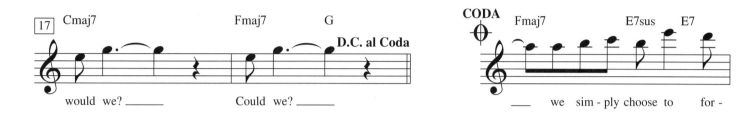

17 | Cmaj7 Fmaj7 G **D.C. al Coda**

would we? _____ Could we? _____

CODA Fmaj7 E7sus E7

___ we sim - ply choose to for -

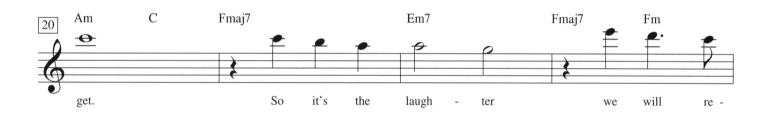

20 | Am C Fmaj7 Em7 Fmaj7 Fm

get. So it's the laugh - ter we will re -

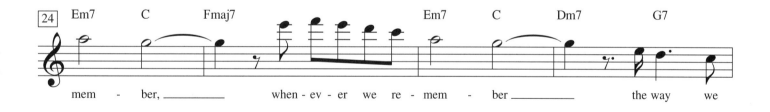

24 | Em7 C Fmaj7 Em7 C Dm7 G7

mem - ber, _____ when - ev - er we re - mem - ber _____ the way we

28 | Cmaj7 Fmaj7 Fm Cmaj7 Fmaj7 Cmaj7

were; the way we were. _____

Can't Help Falling in Love

from the Paramount Picture BLUE HAWAII

Words and Music by George David Weiss,
Hugo Peretti and Luigi Creatore
Arranged by Brenda Dillon

Wise   men   say   on - ly   fools   rush
Shall   I   stay?   Would it   be   a

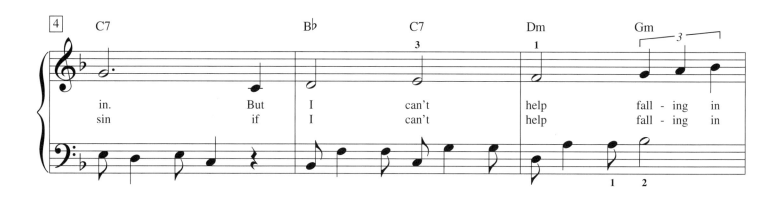

in.   But   I   can't   help   fall - ing   in
sin   if   I   can't   help   fall - ing   in

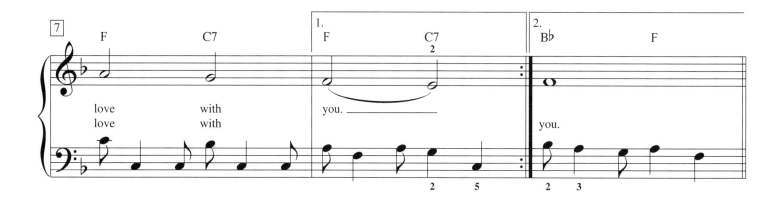

love   with   you. _____
love   with   you.

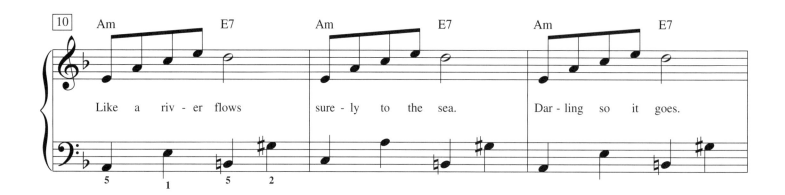

Like a riv - er flows   sure - ly to the sea.   Dar - ling so it goes.

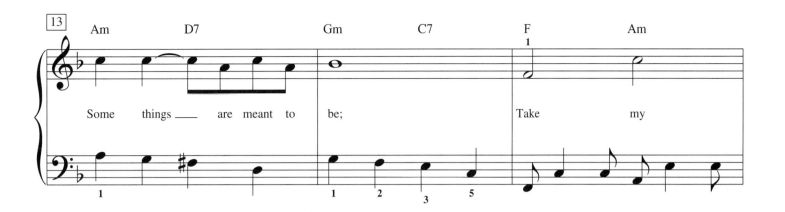

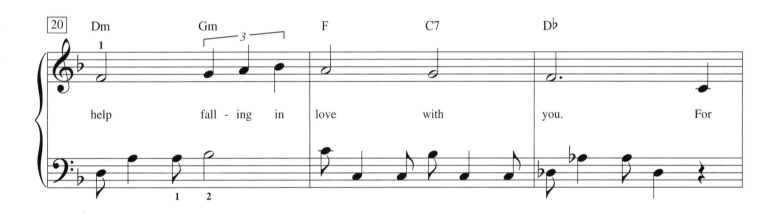

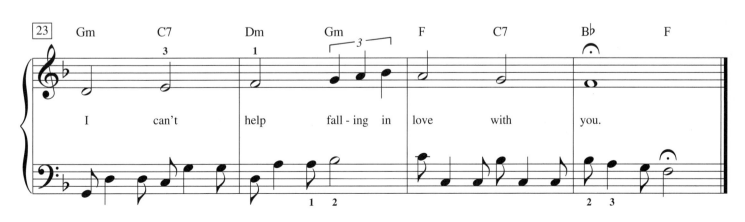

Days of Wine and Roses

from DAYS OF WINE AND ROSES

Lyrics by Johnny Mercer
Music by Henry Mancini
Arranged by Brenda Dillon

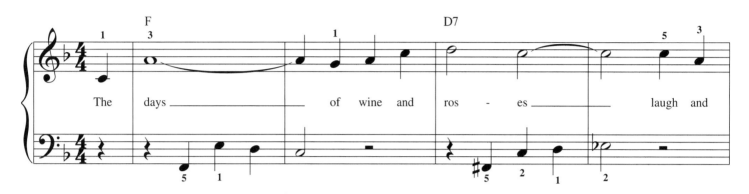

The days _____ of wine and ros - es _____ laugh and

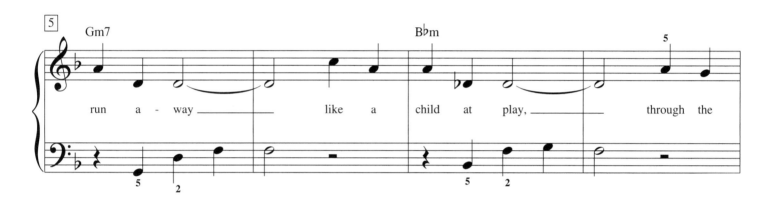

run a - way _____ like a child at play, _____ through the

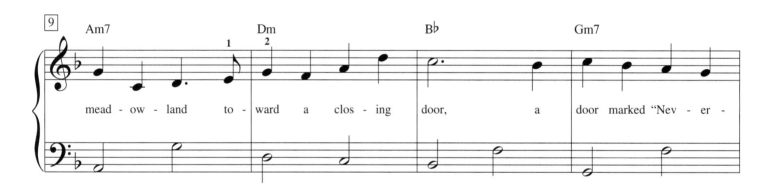

mead - ow - land to - ward a clos - ing door, a door marked "Nev - er -

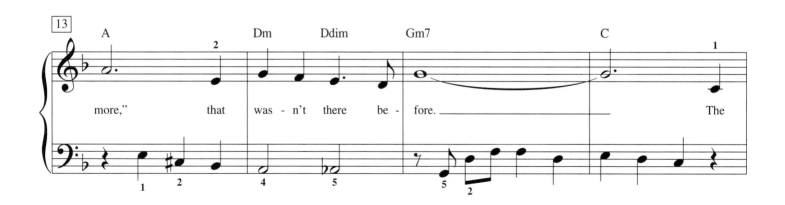

more," that was - n't there be - fore. _____ The

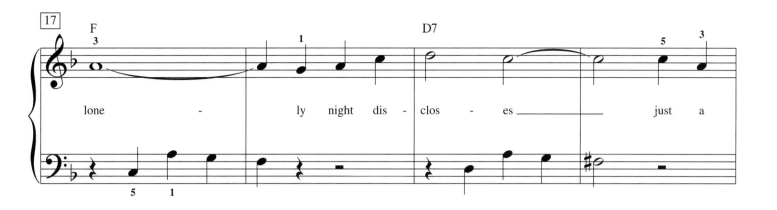

lone - ly night dis - clos - es   just a

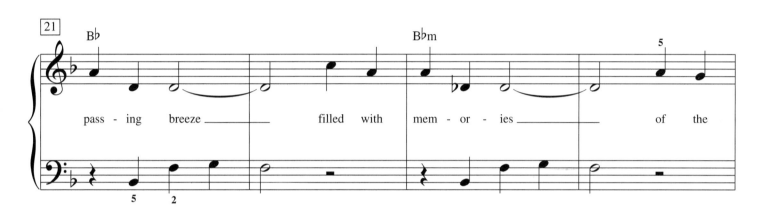

pass - ing breeze   filled with mem - or - ies   of the

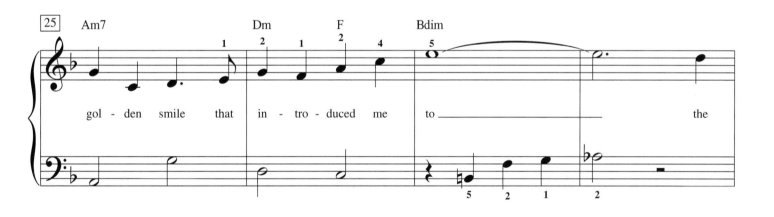

gol - den smile that in - tro - duced me to   the

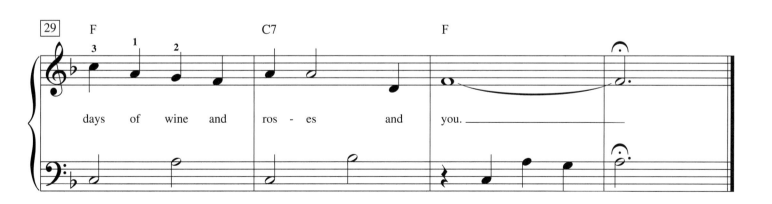

days of wine and ros - es   and   you.

29

Dear Heart
from DEAR HEART

Music by Henry Mancini
Words by Jay Livingston and Ray Evans
Arranged by Brenda Dillon

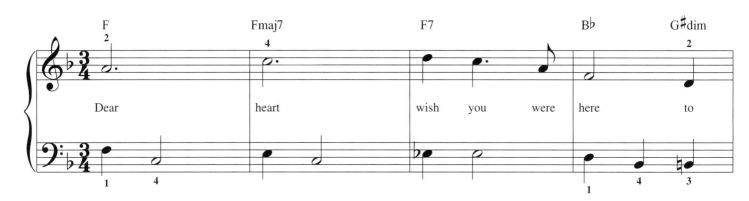

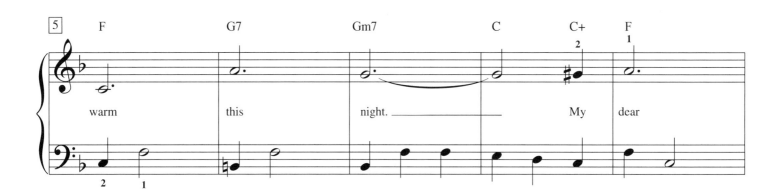

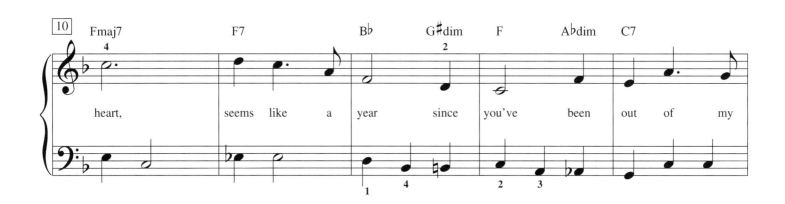

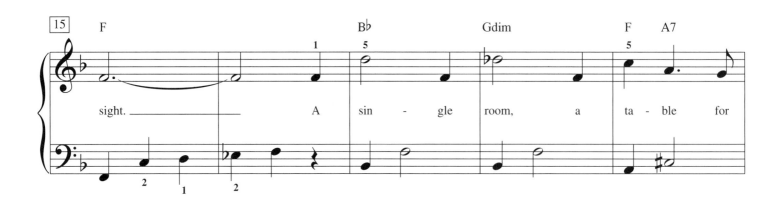

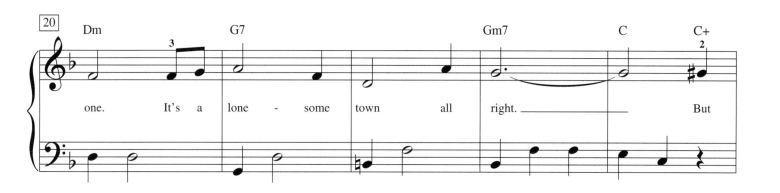

one.   It's a lone - some town all right. _____   But

soon   I'll   kiss you hel - lo   at   our

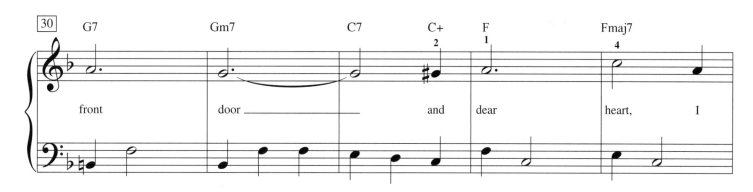

front   door _____   and dear   heart,   I

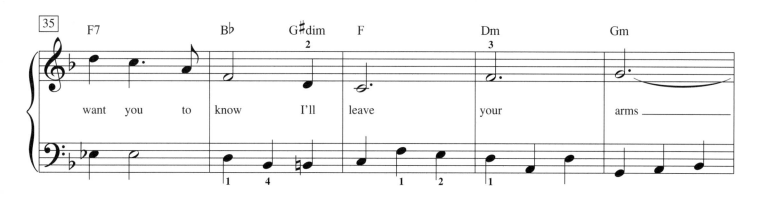

want you to know   I'll leave   your   arms _____

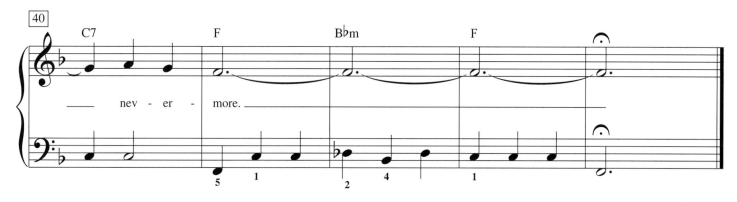

_____ nev - er - more. _____

31

Here's That Rainy Day
from CARNIVAL IN FLANDERS

Words by Johnny Burke
Music by Jimmy Van Heusen

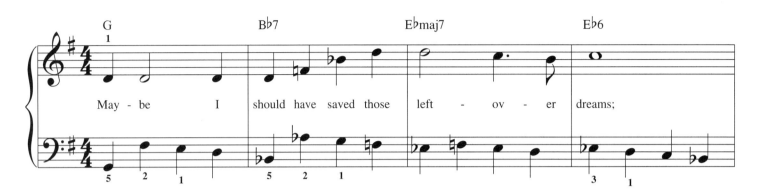

May - be I should have saved those left - ov - er dreams;

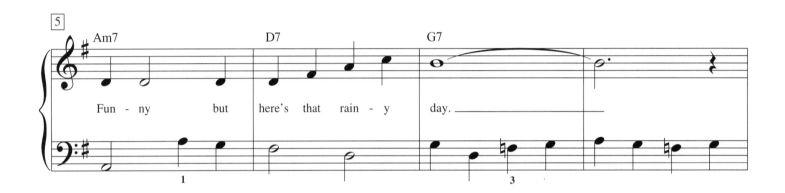

Fun - ny but here's that rain - y day. _____

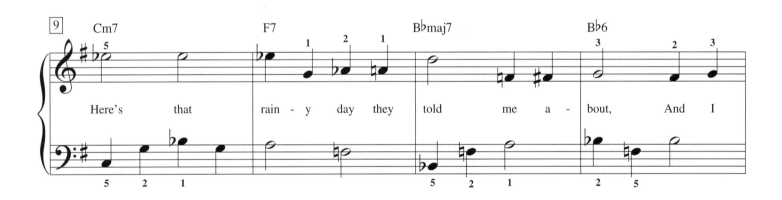

Here's that rain - y day they told me a - bout, And I

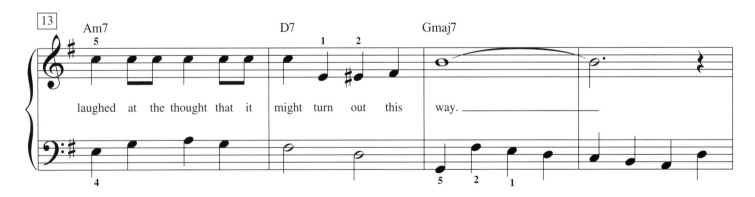

laughed at the thought that it might turn out this way. _____

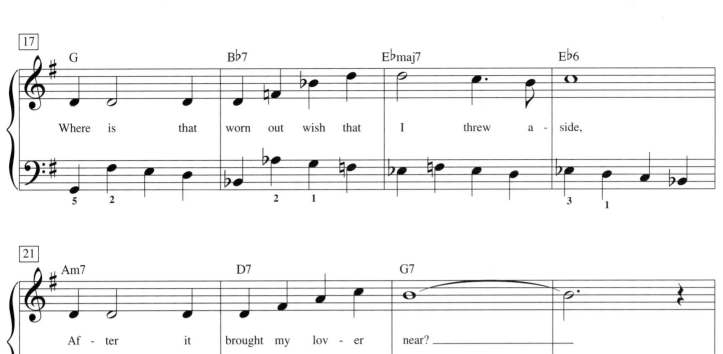

17 G   B♭7   E♭maj7   E♭6

Where is that worn out wish that I threw a - side,

21 Am7   D7   G7

Af - ter it brought my lov - er near? _____

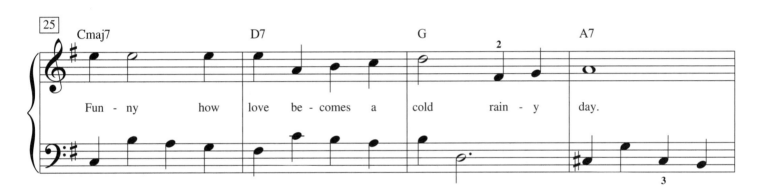

25 Cmaj7   D7   G   A7

Fun - ny how love be - comes a cold rain - y day.

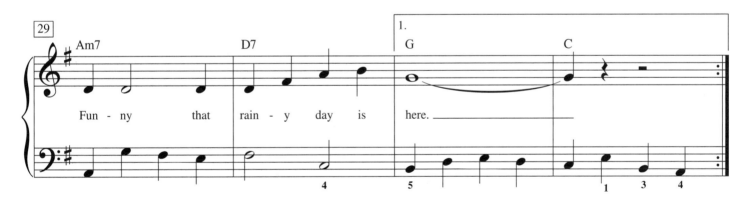

29 Am7   D7   1. G   C

Fun - ny that rain - y day is here. _____

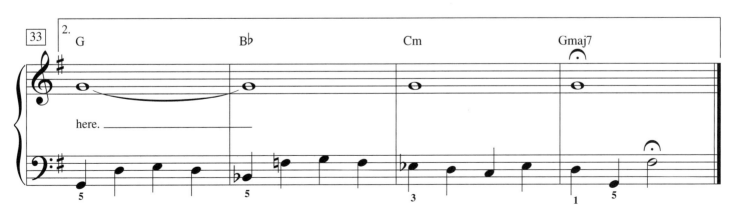

33 2. G   B♭   Cm   Gmaj7

here. _____

It Was Almost Like a Song

Lyric by Hal David
Music by Archie Jordan
Arranged by Brenda Dillon

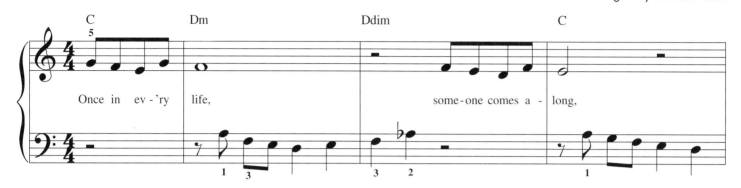

Once in ev-'ry life, some-one comes a - long,

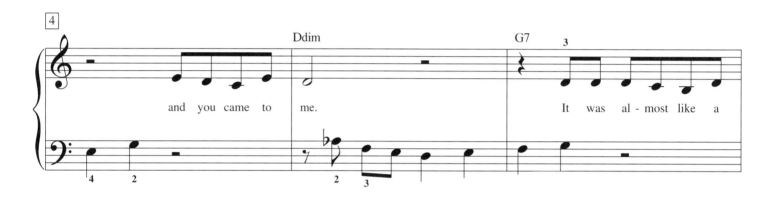

and you came to me. It was al-most like a

song. You were in my arms,

just where you be - long, we were so in

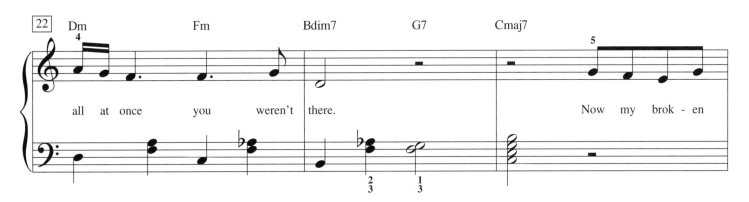

35

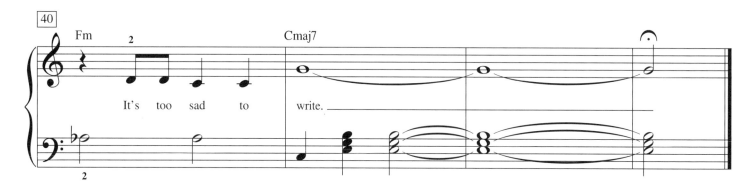

Jean

Words and Music by
Rod McKuen
Arranged by Brenda Dillon

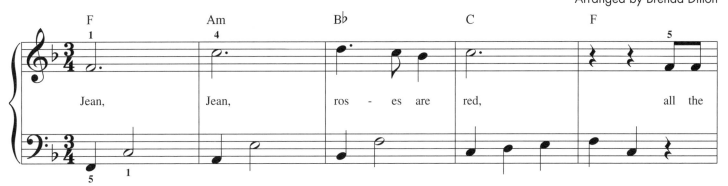

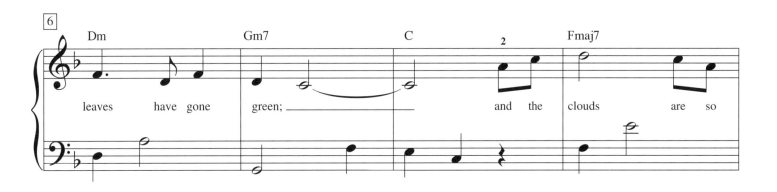

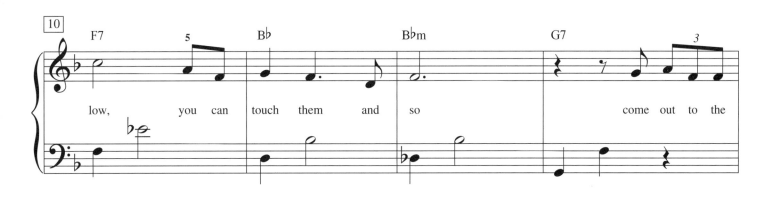

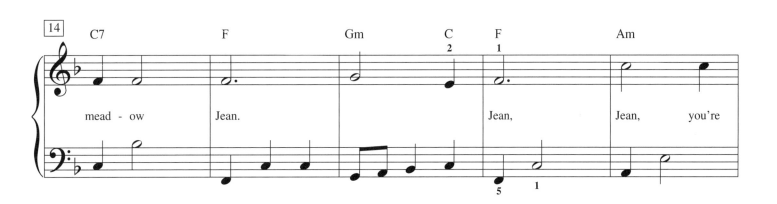

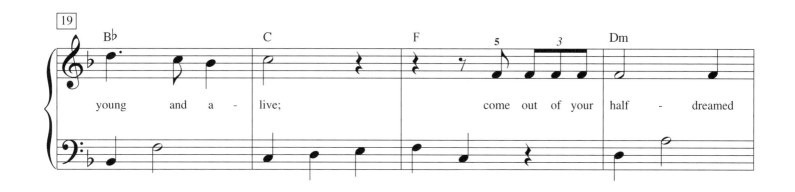

young and a - live; come out of your half - dreamed

dream _____ and run, if you will, to the top of the

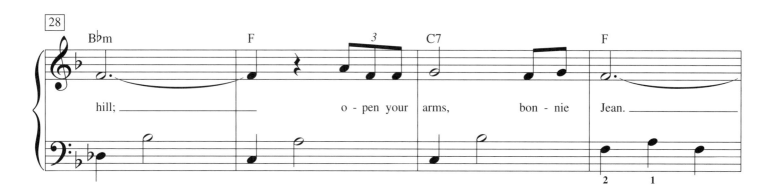

hill; _____ o - pen your arms, bon - nie Jean. _____

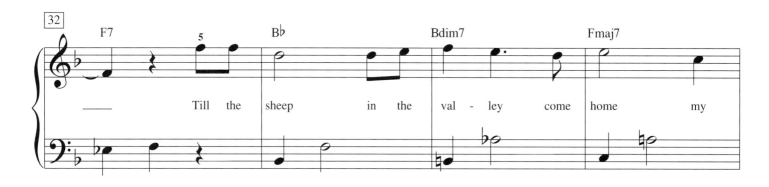

__ Till the sheep in the val - ley come home my

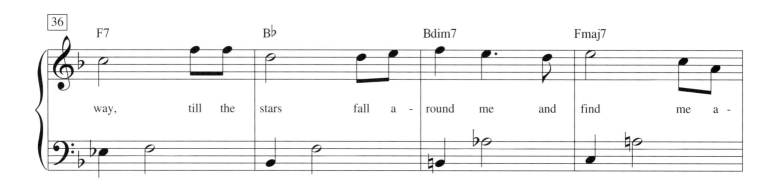

way, till the stars fall a - round me and find me a -

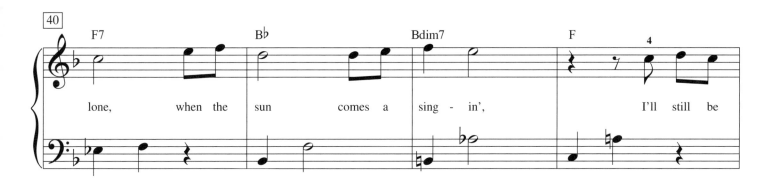

lone,   when the   sun   comes a   sing - in',   I'll still be

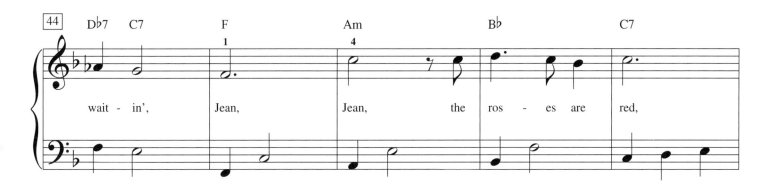

wait - in',   Jean,   Jean,   the ros - es are   red,

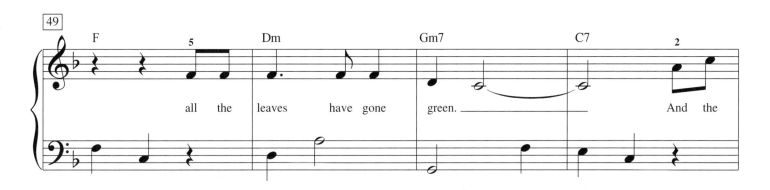

all   the   leaves   have gone   green. _____   And the

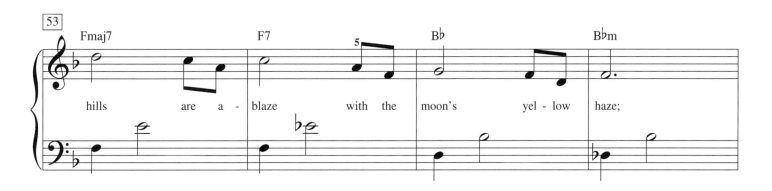

hills   are a - blaze   with the   moon's   yel - low   haze;

come in - to my   arms,   bon - nie   Jean.

My Romance

from JUMBO

Words by Lorenz Hart
Music by Richard Rodgers
Arranged by Brenda Dillon

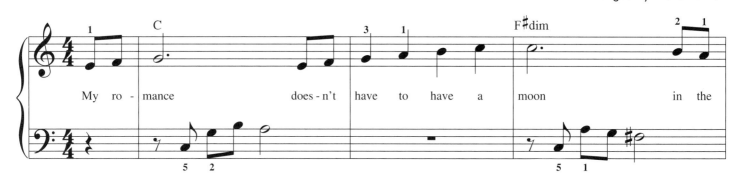

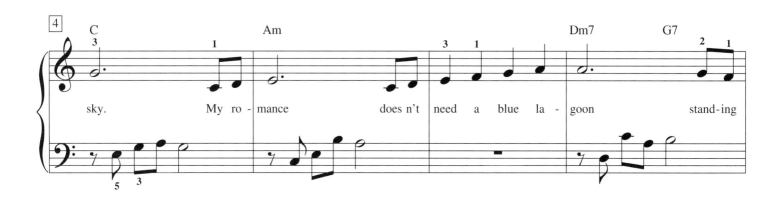

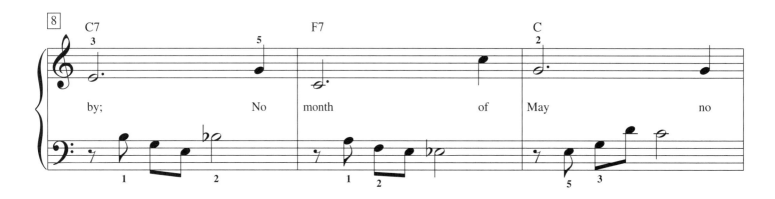

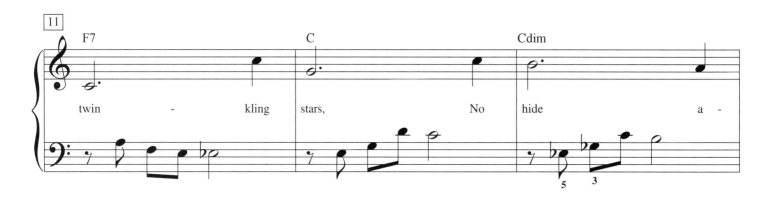

The Shadow of Your Smile
Love Theme from THE SANDPIPER

Music by Johnny Mandel
Words by Paul Francis Webster
Arranged by Brenda Dillon

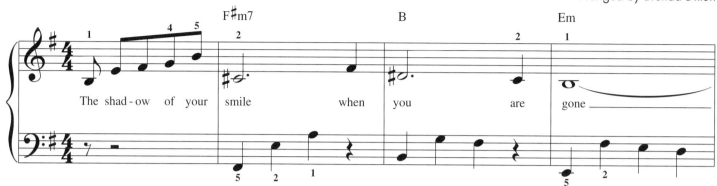

The shad-ow of your smile when you are gone

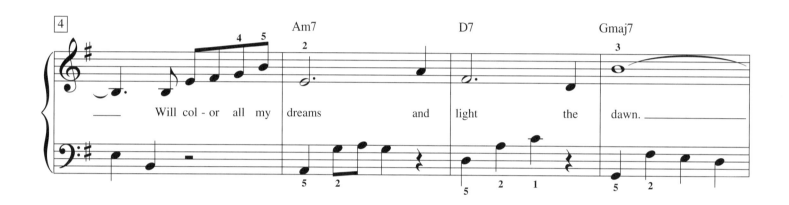

Will col-or all my dreams and light the dawn.

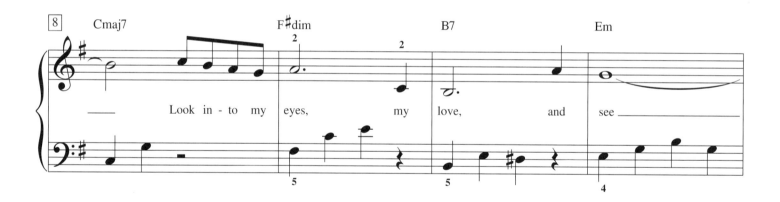

Look in-to my eyes, my love, and see

All the love-ly things you are to me.

Smile
Theme from MODERN TIMES

Words by John Turner and Geoffrey Parsons
Music by Charles Chaplin

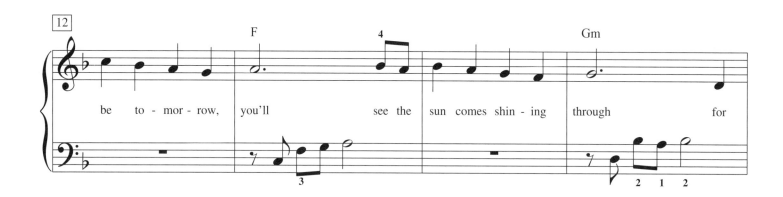

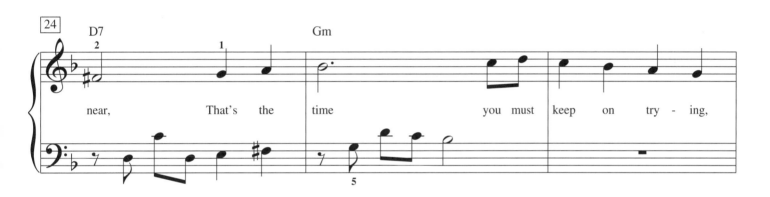

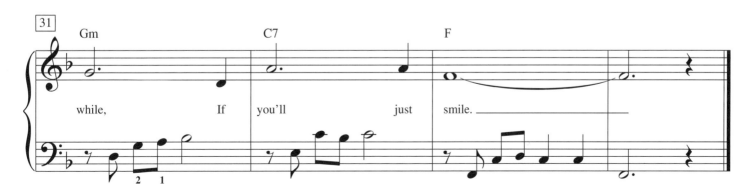

Some Day My Prince Will Come

Words by Larry Morey
Music by Frank Churchill

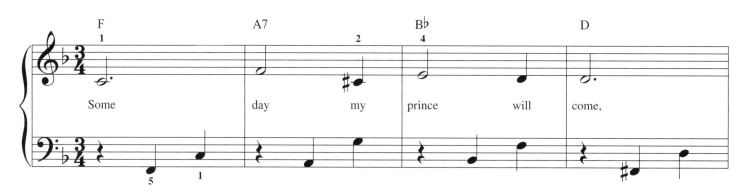

Some day my prince will come,

some day I'll find my love, and how

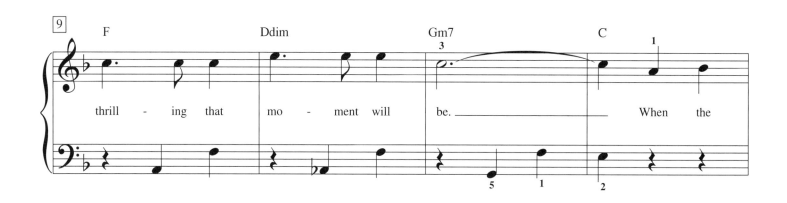

thrill-ing that mo-ment will be. _____ When the

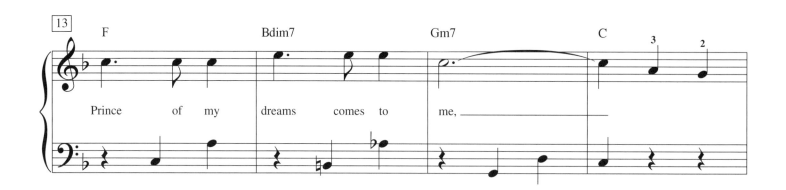

Prince of my dreams comes to me, _____

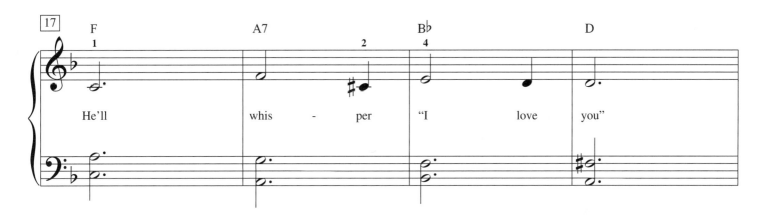

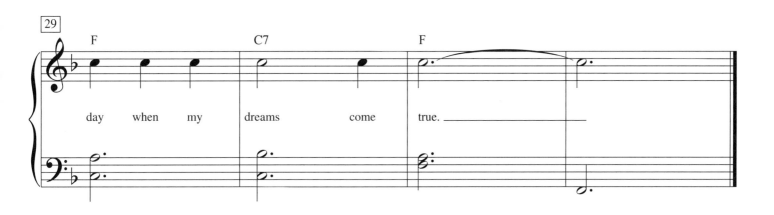

Unchained Melody

Lyric by Hy Zaret
Music by Alex North
Arranged by Brenda Dillon

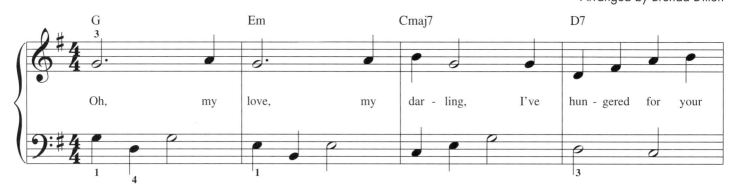

Oh, my love, my dar - ling, I've hun - gered for your

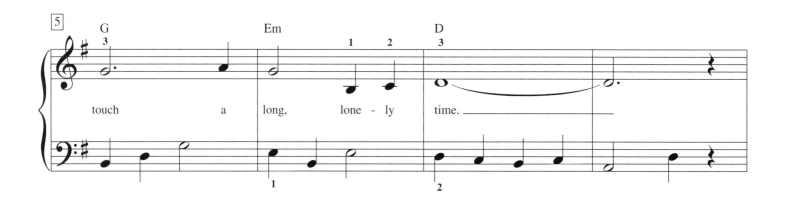

touch a long, lone - ly time. _____

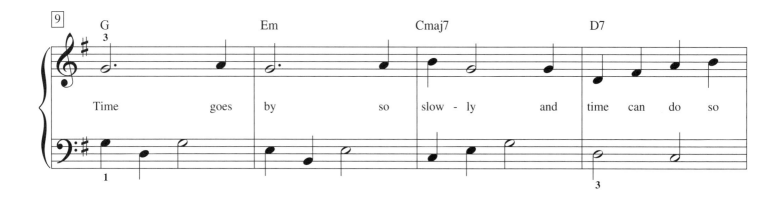

Time goes by so slow - ly and time can do so

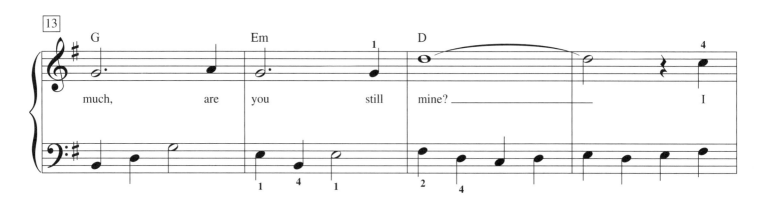

much, are you still mine? _____ I

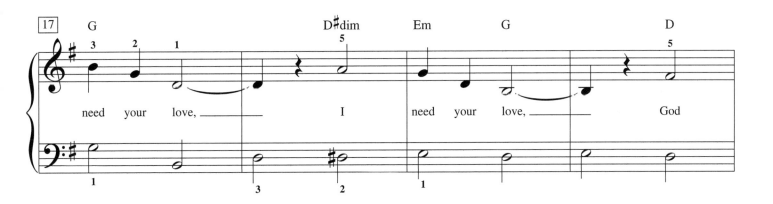

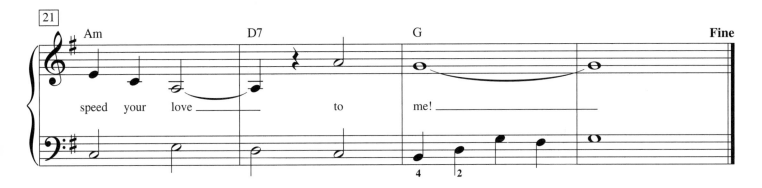

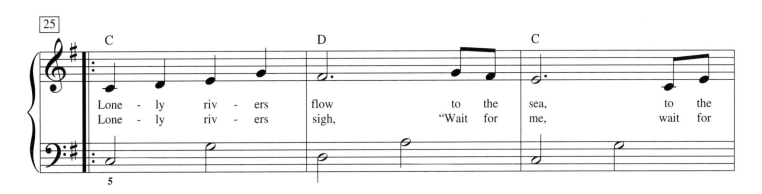

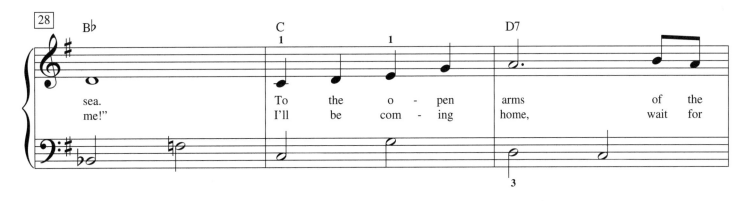

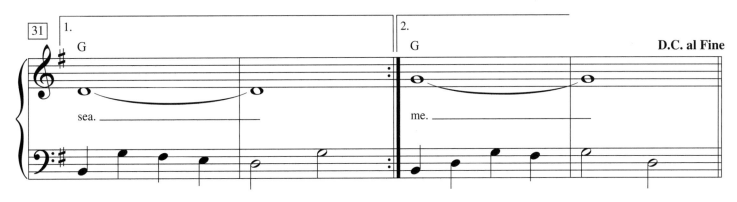

The Way We Were
from the Motion Picture THE WAY WE WERE

Words by Alan and Marilyn Bergman
Music by Marvin Hamlisch
Arranged by Brenda Dillon

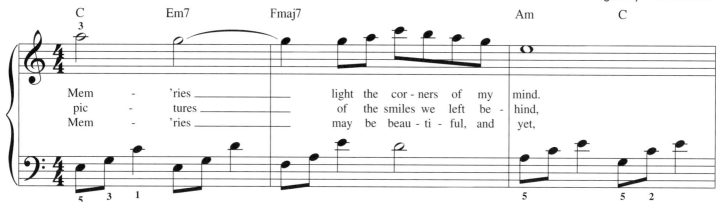

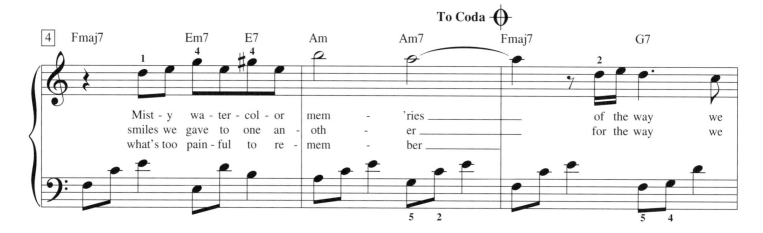

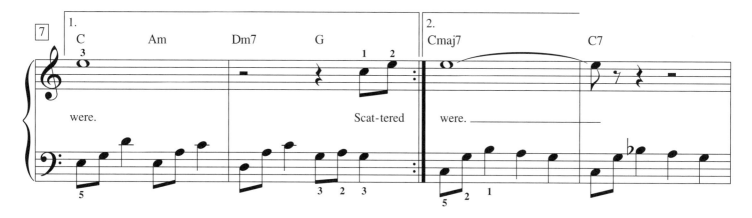

Yesterday

Words and Music by John Lennon
and Paul McCartney
Arranged by Brenda Dillon

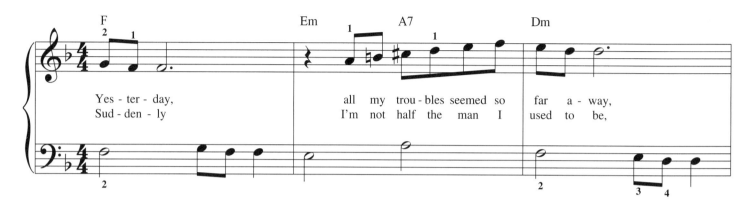

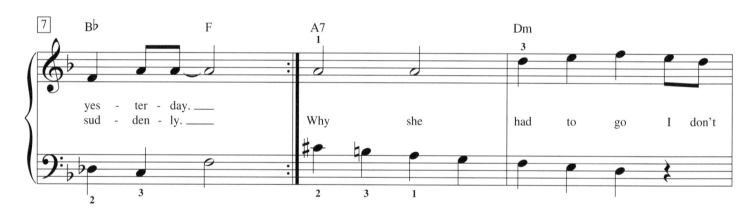

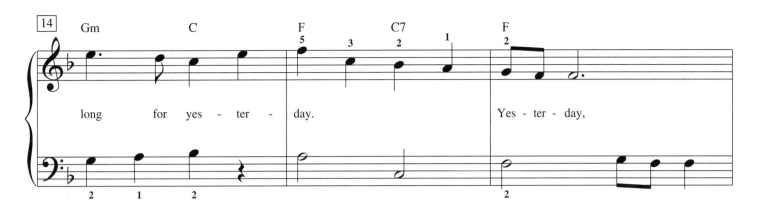

long for yes - ter - day. Yes - ter - day,

love was such an eas - y game to play, now I need a place to

hide a - way, __ Oh I be - lieve __ in yes - ter - day. __

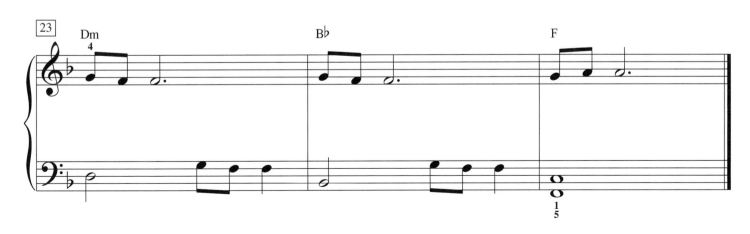

Sunshine on My Shoulders

Words by John Denver
Music by John Denver,
Mike Taylor and Dick Kniss
Arranged by Brenda Dillon

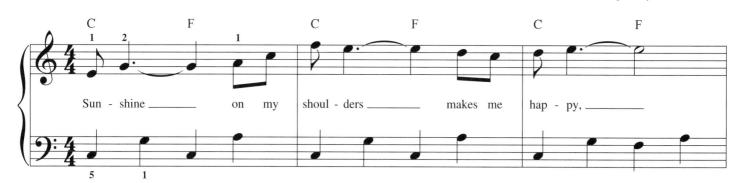

Sun - shine _____ on my shoul - ders _____ makes me hap - py, _____

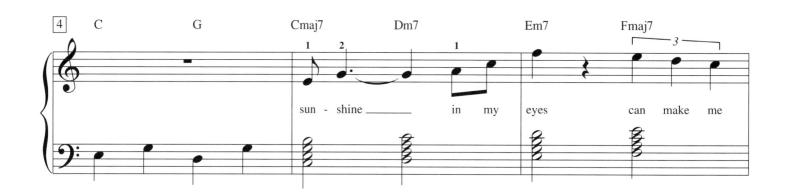

sun - shine _____ in my eyes can make me

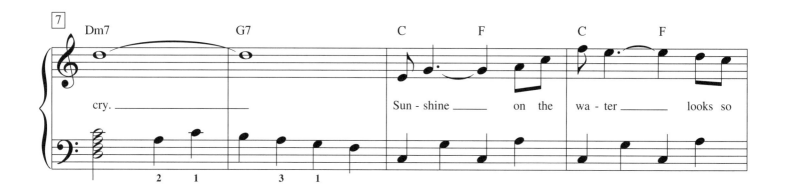

cry. _____ Sun - shine _____ on the wa - ter _____ looks so

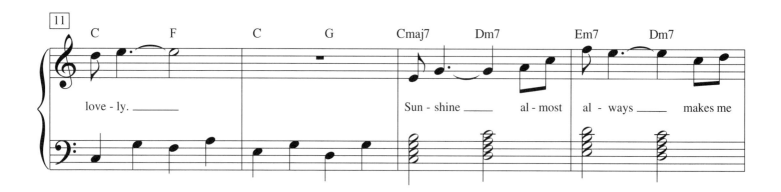

love - ly. _____ Sun - shine _____ al - most al - ways _____ makes me

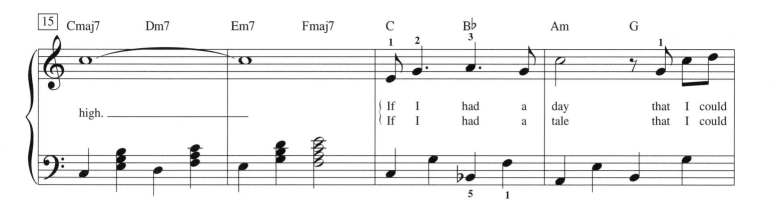

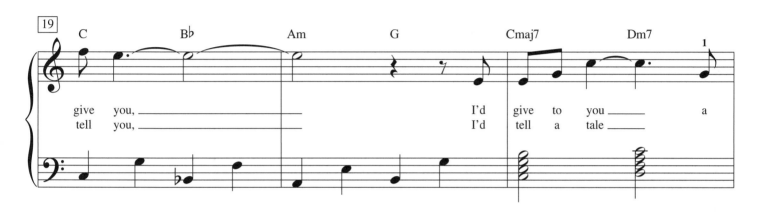

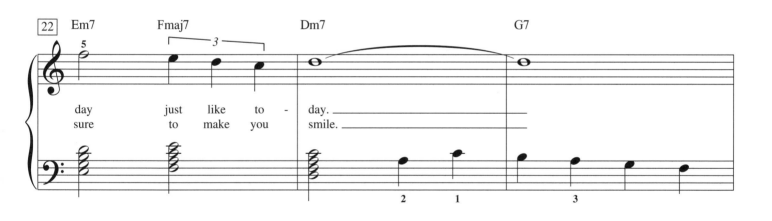

I'd sing a song _____ to make you feel this
I'd make a wish _____ for sun - shine all this

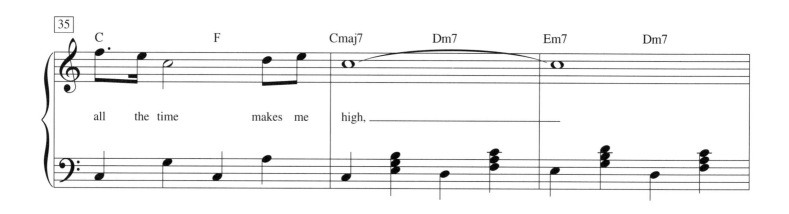

way. _____
while. _____

Sun - shine _____ al - most

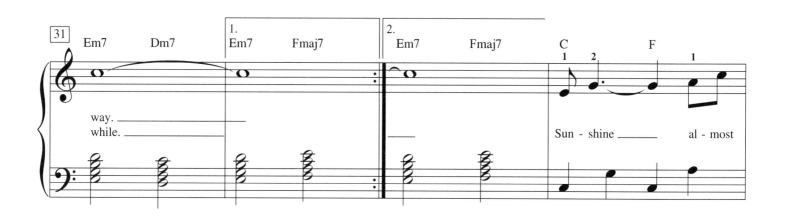

all the time makes me high, _____

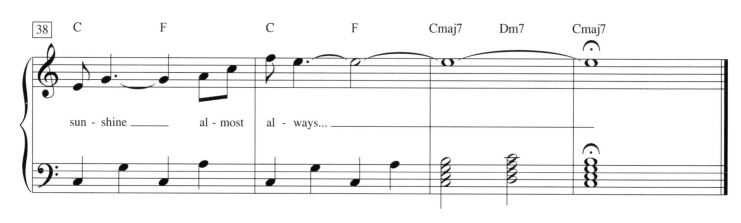

sun - shine _____ al - most al - ways... _____